Leading with Heart
Yene Assegid

LEADING
WITH
HEART

YENE ASSEGID

For my parents

Selemawit Makonnen and Assegid Tessema

I am, because you are

CONTENTS

I

THE BIG PICTURE

In President Barack Obama's eulogy for the American civil rights leader, John Lewis in 2020, he spoke of the importance of humility, kindness and respect for others. He regretted the loss of these values today and their replacement by the trend displayed by so many leaders who seem to "look down" on others rather than lift them up.

The world is hungry for good leadership, for leaders who see themselves as servants of the people, rather than those who lead from ego and who are driven by a desire for self-enrichment. We need leaders who will lead on our behalf, to help improve our lives.

The call is becoming louder now for decency, a return to empathy and compassion and to recognise the humanity of our fellow men and women. These are the qualities exemplified in what I call "leading with heart", a concept we can all practise and one, which, I believe, will make a profound difference in the world.

I recently came across these words and they resonated deeply with my understanding of leadership: 'If service is below you, leadership is beyond you.'

It contradicts a view of leadership as sexy, glitzy and charismatic, the gel in my hair, the right outfit, the wind in my step. It's not. Don't fool yourself. Leadership is about service. It is about finding a purpose that drives you and then pursuing it in the best interest of others. Leadership is about the long run; it's about endurance. Your purpose is something that gets you right in your heart. You get triggered by something and become inspired to follow it; you can't help it. You don't wake up one day and say, 'I want to be a leader.' You can't; it's not possible. When you lead and you lead well, it's because you care about something so much that even if you're the only one standing, you're going to do it. Some people will try to burst your bubble, but you know what you are doing and why you're doing it and that's what keeps you going.

If you really want to lead in the world, you need to be clear about your purpose. The first thing is why do you do what you do? What is the purpose? What's the meaning you get out of it? You can't lead well, you can't sustain it unless you really care about something and you really feel it in your gut, even if you're talking about leading within a company, or within an organisation. If you work for a company that you don't care for, quit. Get another job; let somebody else do that job. If you're not happy in the role that you have there, stop it. Find a role that you like; one that makes you keep going even when you feel tired. This is the value of finding your purpose, what makes you happy, because if you really know what makes you happy, you can't do anything else. That is what really has the most meaning for you.

So the first thing is to be clear about your purpose. What makes you happy, what gives you meaning? And please have the courage to pick that up. You know what, God is not going to send you an email or a registered letter to say, 'Oh my son or my daughter, or so and so I would like you to go and do this.' No, it's whispers. These are the whispers that wake you up in the middle of the night and inspire you. People ask me, 'But how will I know?' You will know that you're not in the sweet spot when you're not in the sweet spot. You know it's not sweet; you'll be bored. Do you want to live your life like that? Find something that drives you. It's what you would rather die trying to achieve than not to try at all.

When you find what it is you want to do and why you want to do it, get started. How do you do it? You can't change things alone, by yourself. You need people to come with you; you need to share your dreams, you need to share your vision and allow others to make it their own. And as you work with people, keep them inspired, not only those in your group and in your organisation but people you don't even know yet. The more you can energise others with your vision, the more people will want to become a part of it. It's all about your style of leadership and how you make others feel.

Fortunately and unfortunately there are many theories and models of leadership for us to follow. Have a look at them once your purpose is activated. When you get your fire going you can choose a model and theory on which to base your leadership capacity and carve out your own style.

Some years back I was in Johannesburg, South Africa to interview various leaders for my studies. I met with Constitutional Court Judge Yvonne Mokgoro in her office in a downtown building which had been constructed from some of the bricks taken from Number Four Prison which once held Nelson Mandela, Robert Sobukwe and Mahatma Gandhi, as well as thousands of ordinary prisoners.

The Constitutional Court stood as a symbol of human rights in South Africa and Judge Mokgoro told me that every day when she went to work, she thought about those who had suffered to bring about a new country. As I listened to her, I could not stop weeping. My heart fell apart both for the pain so many had endured on that site and for the magnificent transformation the new space represented.

Judge Mokgoro was kind and said she would arrange another interview for me, with someone she described as 'the busiest man'. I was only in the country for a week from my base in Sierra Leone and I crossed my fingers tightly that it would work out. It did. I was given an appointment for that Tuesday at eight thirty a.m. I arrived a whole ninety minutes early at the reception in a beautiful modern building. Around eight a.m. his personal assistant came to the conference room where I had been asked to wait and told me that he could unfortunately now only give me fifteen minutes as his day had filled up.

She ushered me into a boardroom where I placed myself at a gleaming long table, on one side of a glass wall. I positioned my recording gear, which I had tested and retested, and sat looking through the glass out into the corridor. At precisely eight-thirty a.m. in walked a man dressed business casual, in a black sweater, black pants and a classic shirt peeking through the sweater. He had kind eyes. He greeted me warmly and sat down opposite me. I nervously placed my mic and recorder nearer to him assuring him, 'I won't take much of your time. My questions are ready.' As I was about to press the record button, he motioned with his hand and said: 'It's okay, slow down. Tell me a little bit about yourself and why you do what you do.' This threw me slightly and before I could think, I blurted out: 'It started when I was born.' I could not believe I had said that. The man had only fifteen minutes to give me and I went right back to the time of my birth.

As I shared my life story and why I was working on the topic of leadership, he smiled and listened. At times he chuckled at some of my stories. The more he listened, the more I shared and I lost track of time completely. It felt to me like I was talking with someone I had known for many years, like an uncle or a family friend.

Since he had his back to the glass wall, he didn't notice his PA hovering about and checking her watch, but I saw her out of the corner of my eye. I knew she would soon interrupt us but I was still sharing, telling him about myself and why I do what I do. About forty-five minutes later, she came into the room to whisk him away and I realised I had not recorded a single thing. I was devastated. Here I was with a rare interview opportunity and I had wasted it by sharing my childhood stories and not recording what he had to say. 'Can I make another appointment?' I asked, almost pleading. 'Maybe Saturday? I return to Freetown in less than a week and it will be difficult to come back soon.' He replied, 'I am sorry, Saturday is a full day. But don't worry, now that we know each other we can work together.'

All I could do was to surrender and agree. Despite his PA wanting him to follow her to his next appointment, he walked with me outside to the waiting car and even insisted on helping me wheel my heavy briefcase across the parking area. 'It was good to meet you', he repeated, greeted the driver and warmly bid me farewell.

A few days later I received a call from a man working with an organisation of former heads of state in Africa who I had met through President Kenneth Kaunda of Zambia. He invited me to join him and his group the next day to plant trees at a hospital in Soweto in honour of Nelson Mandela's birthday. I accepted right away and asked if I could bring Kelo, the friend I was staying with. On the Saturday morning, she and I showed up at their hotel to join their motorcade.

After the tree planting ceremony, the motorcade headed away from the city to a high-end residential area. As we turned into a street lined with parked cars, we noticed an unusual amount of movement for a Saturday and what looked like high-level security. I caught a glimpse of the shock on Kelo's face. 'Oh my God, we are heading to Madiba's house', she whispered. Sure enough, it was Nelson Mandela's home. We followed the delegation into the house. The living room was full of guests; and I did not know a single person except for Kelo. And then it happened; I heard my name being called out loudly from the other side of the room. I thought I was hallucinating. Who could ever know my name in this place? I turned around to see the man I had interviewed on Tuesday morning. 'Yene, it's so good to see you', he said. 'Come with me;

let me introduce you to my friends.' I followed him and met many people. I guess he meant it when he had said at our first meeting, 'Now that we know each other we can work together.'

As much as I regretted not having had a recording of our conversation, it all began to make sense. He had given me a leadership lesson wrapped in a series of events that unfolded that week in Johannesburg. Take time to connect, to get to know and to understand others; this relatedness is what will allow us to create a strong foundation on which we can work better together. It's the difference between collecting a stack of business cards from people we forget almost instantly and having memories of a meaningful conversation with someone. This is what matters, our capacity to relate to one another; our capacity to know that behind our titles, jobs and roles is a human being. It is that human being that we need to relate to. The rest is not important. When we relate well to that human being, we can move mountains together.

Incidentally, the businessman Judge Mokgoro had arranged for me to meet that day was Cyril Ramaphosa, a celebrated anti-apartheid leader who later went on to serve as the President of South Africa. At the time of our interview, he was a successful businessman with a stake in several multi-million dollar companies. He could have just taken my few questions and gone through the allocated fifteen minutes without a blink. Instead he took his time. He listened to me. He treated me like a dear guest, a sister and a daughter. He didn't have to do that. But he did. The point is that those of us who recognise the human dignity of other people, rather than their position in life, their wealth or lack of wealth, are the kinds of leaders that make a difference. They touch the lives of ordinary people and make real transformation possible.

II

MY SEARCH FOR LEADERSHIP

One thing we all know for sure is that the world has changed dramatically and it will keep on changing in ways that we can't always anticipate. The year 2020 felt to so many of us as if the giant carpet holding us in place had been ripped out from under our feet. It was terrifying not to know if we would suffer the potentially devastating effects of a Covid-19 infection or if we would even live to tell the tale.

When we sit down with our grandparents and other elders, we hear their stories of the massive changes in their lifetime and in the lives of their parents and grandparents. This is the nature of life. Every so often something huge comes along that wipes away our security, shakes up our hopes and replaces them with fear and uncertainty. Many of our elders and ancestors lived through at least one war, a pandemic or an economic depression. Sometimes all three.

My own first real crisis, which set me off on a dramatic new trajectory, came in the form of revolution in the country of my birth, Ethiopia.

Incessant banging on our bedroom window late one night announced to my sister Fofi and I that everything had changed forever. The rapping on the glass was accompanied by screaming, so loud that it dragged us from our sleep. Hussein was yelling at us to 'Open the door! Open, quickly!' Dressed in our white "Hello Sweetie" nightgowns we little girls cautiously padded in our bare feet into the living room. Peering through the glass door and into the darkness outside, I could make out more than one person and, at first, I thought the shadowy figures were my Aunt Koky and her husband Yigezu. He was a pilot and often used to bring her to our house early in the morning when he had to fly out of Bole Airport. But as my eyes adjusted to the murkiness outside I saw that, instead of the familiar outlines of my aunt and uncle, there stood six or seven soldiers in their army fatigues, filling the frame of the outside world.

Almost as soon as we opened the door, we saw a shotgun pointed straight at us. I can still remember my shock as I stared into the barrel of a rifle aimed at my face. House raids had become common in Addis Ababa where soldiers would randomly search homes or because someone had reported a family to the kebeles, the community authorities. We didn't know if this time it was "just a search", or if it would end with an arrest or even the execution of someone found to be "against the revolution" – we children had often heard the adults whispering details of such frightening events.

In their search for "imperialist materials", the soldiers hauled clothes from our closets, tipped out the contents of drawers and tore pictures from the walls of our home and left it looking as if a storm had ripped through it. That raid was not the same as others we had experienced before. It pierced a hole right through the centre of our world and eventually led to us leaving our country and becoming eternal migrants. To us, being wrenched from our family and all that was familiar, it felt as if the world had come to an end, but I learned much later that there was nothing so exceptional about it. I had become just one of the million or so people a year who are forced to leave their homes due to war, persecution or conflict. I became one of them when my parents packed us up and took my sisters and I from Ethiopia to Belgium. We escaped the Derg – the junta that had overthrown the Emperor, Haile Selassie and which went on to murder tens of thousands of people and, infamously, to ignore a famine in which over a million people perished.

I did not have to endure the physical hardships of so many migrants today; I survived but I ended up as a stranger in a strange land. My whole world then was school and my grandmother's compound, nothing else. Being forced to flee, at the age of ten, sent me on two journeys: a physical one and an internal one. I began to dream of a world in which people would not have to leave their homes, their towns or their motherlands. It made me realise that at the heart of the enforced movement of people, was leadership. When leadership is not exercised for the people, when it is self-centred, society will start to unravel. Conflict and chaos result and can often lead to ordinary people seeking a life elsewhere.

Leaving is not always an option for everyone; an entire community cannot simply up and go, splitting from those we love the most and from what we know. You pack, you go; sometimes you don't even pack, you just go, never sure of seeing your loved ones again or even finding them should you return one day. So we hand our fate over to a higher power and move on. Our leaving was relatively easy in the sense that our journey to a safe place was not a perilous one at the mercy of people smugglers, across wild waters in small vessels or stuffed into the back of trucks. But we did not escape the emotional and economic scars left when we uprooted ourselves.

For me, leaving still evokes a particular physical reaction. When I recall our departure from Ethiopia, a bitter taste rises in the back of my throat and pulls on my gut; a tingling creeps into my body and my heart races. Half a century later, whenever I leave a place that I have lived, I have to take a deep breath and negotiate with my emotions. To calm myself I focus on the knowledge that nothing is permanent and that all things will pass, just as I, too, will pass one day.

Leaving my country left me feeling empty and lost and my tiny frightened internal voice kept asking me, 'What now?' I had no answers then. It took me years to untangle this jumble of emotions until I was finally able to make the best out of the cards I had been dealt. I began to draw lessons from my own life and experiences and found that the best way to make sense of my experiences was to take what I had learned and share it with as many people as possible; to be there for others, to help people whose lives had also been thrown into turmoil. My quest evolved into working with people who want to find a way forward, to figure out how to lead their own lives and then the best way to lead others.

I felt that I would never get back the familiar warm sense of belonging I had growing up. Moving from a country in which almost everyone was black, to a world where I did not look the same as most people around me, I discovered a sense of unbelonging. At best, I would always be seen as a visitor, a guest who had overstayed her welcome and whenever I returned to my country, I would always be the "returnee". Such is my life and the lives of countless others who have had to leave their countries looking for peace, safety and opportunities elsewhere. I became a global nomad, having to make the best of the situation, while trying to understand what led my own family and so many other families to be displaced, to emigrate, to be uprooted from their homes.

I came to the conclusion that it all came down to a lack of good leadership, a lack of leadership in service of the people. I understood that leaders would either step up in times of crisis to help the whole community or they chose instead to only look after themselves and their close circle. It became clear to me that ego-driven leadership lies at the root of so much of what goes wrong. Often the more selfish a leader is, the narrower their worldview, the less evolved their consciousness and the more insecure they are about their own power. It made me wonder what would happen if we could each develop our own expression of leadership and what could be its impact? Much later on I decided to focus my doctoral work on a study of this power to see for myself how leading well could transform people's lives for the better.

I spent time with about thirty leading figures from twelve countries to unpack how they made their own leadership work. I hoped that from these elders I would be able to distil a set of lessons, a blueprint of how to lead well. Among them were freedom fighters, trade unionists, opinion makers and spiritual leaders. I sat with them, quietly soaking up their wisdom as they answered my questions through simple and moving anecdotes. It felt like a sacred experience, even when we sat in silence as they searched for the best way to express a point. Amongst those I interviewed were Kofi Annan of Ghana, Ahmed Kathrada of South Africa, Ibrahim Mayaki of Niger and Joséphine Ouédraogo of Burkina Faso. I left each meeting with these unassuming and visionary individuals feeling more inspired and hopeful that indeed, selfless leadership was possible.

Kofi Annan, an international civil servant, had served two terms as the secretary general of the United Nations from 1997 to 2006, and was the co-recipient, with the United Nations, of the Nobel Prize for Peace in 2001. Ahmed Kathrada was one of seven men sentenced to life imprisonment with Nelson Mandela on 12 June 1964 for their fight to end South Africa's racist system of apartheid. He spent twenty-six years in prison and emerged to serve in his country's first democratically elected parliament.

Ibrahim Mayaki, the transitional Prime Minister of Niger, from 1997 to 2000, was the CEO of the New Partnership for Africa's Development (NEPAD), an economic development programme of the African Union. Joséphine Ouédraogo served in the government of Burkina Faso, on the invitation of that country's revolutionary and iconic leader, Thomas Sankara and went on to a career in various international organisations.

I wanted to interview people who, in their own way, had faced a range of challenges and who had triumphed. I wanted to discover their secrets to leading well, and how they stayed on track without losing their own humanity in the process. I came away with a handful of lessons we can all absorb into our lives and behaviour, no matter who we are or what level of leadership we occupy. These leaders and their stories inspired me to use every ounce of my energy to help people learn to lead in service of others, no matter the size of their orbit of influence. I believe that it is real transformation that will improve the lives of every person and ultimately make the world a better place. This has become my calling.

Spending time with these elders showed me that above all else, whoever we lead we can learn to do it well.

III

THE LESSONS

One day, while I was drawing up a list of which leaders I could interview for my research, my father casually suggested, 'Why don't you talk to Kofi?' I just smiled. All my life I had marvelled at my father's approach; nothing ever seemed impossible for him. His mantra was, 'You can only try.' At best it will happen and in the worst case it won't happen. You have nothing to lose if you try. Back in the early sixties my father was one of the few Africans studying at the Graduate Institute of International and Development Studies in Geneva, Switzerland. He was doing his doctoral studies in International Law and Political Science and Kofi Annan, who had come from the United States to do his master's, was one of his best friends there. Since then, of course, their lives had gone in different directions. My father pursued a life in international business and Kofi Annan joined the United Nations Economic Commission for Africa (UNECA). Before I could even answer my father he had decided, 'Let me see how I can get in touch with him.'

Within days we were on a train from Brussels to Geneva via Paris. I love travelling with my father;

I become a little girl again and once again he is my father, my hero. We shared an amazing meal at an Ethiopian restaurant on our first evening in Geneva and the next day we were waiting in the reception of the office of the retired UN secretary general, Kofi Annan. The first I saw of him was a beaming smile lighting up the familiar face, and then his outstretched arms moving in to embrace my father. 'It's been years, Assegid', he exclaimed. Then it was my turn and I was greeted in the way one receives the child of an old friend. I felt as if I was being escorted to my first day at school with my father holding my hand. We sat around the office and the two old friends chatted about the past, catching up on the present. Then Kofi Annan turned to me and asked: 'What can I do for you?' I explained; and he shared with me the challenges he had faced at the United Nations. I listened, absorbed; I took notes. What I saw was not his titles and world fame, but a human being who had been thoroughly tested and how he had dealt with those challenges.

At the end of the interview he asked me, 'How old are you, Yene?' The question came from left field. I thought, 'Oh my gosh, I am forty years old – he will think I am such a failure.' I had no big career to present. I had had a few jobs in international organisations but nothing to write home about. All I had done was to raise my daughters, and was then working on my PhD.

With a slight sense of panic gripping my heart, I blurted out, 'I am forty years old.' He smiled. 'You are doing really well, Yene. Continue what you are doing. It's important work. It takes time. Don't be discouraged. Just keep on keeping on', he said. I bathed in his words as if they were the reassuring morning sunlight.

When it came time to end the meeting I thanked him for making the time for me. I said, 'Thanks to you I was able to spend two full days alone with my father. It's been fantastic.' He laughed out loud and said, 'Now I know you know what really matters in life. If you ever need anything else, you know where I am.' He walked us all the way to the door and we said goodbye.

My appointment to see Ahmed Kathrada was set for eight thirty a.m. at his apartment in Johannesburg. Again, I arrived early, around seven a.m. While waiting in the lobby of his building I called the person who arranged the meeting to let her know I was there already. Within minutes she called me back to say I could go up – he was ready to meet me.

He answered the door himself and made me a cup of tea before we moved through to his bright living room and started the interview thirty minutes early. We took that extra time and more as he painted a picture of his activism from childhood, imprisonment and freedom. Talking to "Mr K", a term of affection used by many of the people close to him, I wished I could have increased the size of my ears to listen more. What he shared with me was so incredibly vivid that I sat with chills through the whole interview.

Leadership is not learned he told me, it comes with a baptism of fire, or what he liked to say was rather 'a baptism of cold water'. Here sat one of South Africa's liberation heroes modestly recounting story after story of the challenges he had faced in his eventful life and how he had overcome them. One tale that bore deep into my heart was one he told about when he arrived at a prison in the depths of winter and, with other prisoners, was ordered to strip naked and to take a shower in the courtyard. He was then a young man who had lived a comfortable life and had never before had to take a cold shower. The prison guards stood around mocking them as he and his comrades showered in ice-cold water in the open air. Mr K showered as quickly as possible but the guards forced him to return, to do it again. As he walked back in the icy winter air towards what he knew would be unbearably cold water, he decided that he would control the situation. Mr K told me that suddenly he did not feel freezing; he stood under the shower without moving and vowed that he would stand there until the guards themselves could not stand watching him anymore. He stood, and stood, and stood under the cold water. In this magnificent demonstration of quiet resistance, he showed them that he was in control of the situation, not them.

This story made me think of how we protect ourselves from being tested; we shield ourselves from pain. Yet, it's when we go through pain and stand tall in the face of challenges that we sharpen our leadership. All we have to do is to allow ourselves, our inner deepest selves, to trust and know that we will make it through.

I interviewed Dr Ibrahim Mayaki in Dakar, Senegal where he was running Rural Hub, an organisation to support development in West and Central Africa. He had previously served as the transitional Prime Minister of Niger. This former university professor had lost his close friend, Niger President Ibrahim Baré Maïnassara in a military coup and his own father was in jail for much of the time he was growing up.

He told me how throughout his father's imprisonment, the family's gardener had served as a father figure to him and had supported, protected and helped the family as if they were his own. Each day, the gardener would deliver food to Dr Mayaki's father in prison. When he was released he was found to be seriously ill and the family discovered that throughout the years they had sent him the food, the prison guards regularly added finely ground glass to it before giving it to his father.

What I took away from that interview was that we should never give up, that we continue on in honour of those who fell along the way; and we must ensure that their lives were not in vain. Dr Mayaki impressed on me that we must keep believing in our vision and look forward while always remembering what it has taken to get us this far.

At the end of our conversation, he told me he was travelling to Johannesburg to take up a new post. I only found out later that this post was as the chief executive officer of NEPAD. This is the type of humility that distinguishes those who lead for a purpose from those who are in it for their own ego.

I first met Joséphine Ouédraogo in 1998 when I was running a programme for Médecins Sans Frontières (MSF) on HIV/AIDS prevention in the red light district of Addis Ababa. I still had that magical energy of youth and would spend ten-hour days in the office and be with the women until past midnight most nights. Mme Ouédraogo was the director of Women and Gender for the United Nations Economic Commission for Africa (UNECA). I went to see her to tell her what my colleagues and I in MSF were doing for women.

Just as I would experience with the other leaders, she received me as if I was the most important person she had met. I was wearing jeans and a basic linen shirt and had dust on my shoes; but she welcomed me like she would a VIP. Many years later, I interviewed her for my PhD in Dakar where she was the secretary general of the NGO, Environment Development Action in the Third World (ENDA). I was struck by her message that while we sometimes assume that we operate in a vacuum, we all carry the wisdom of our ancestors and elders. She said we should keep in mind that we are not alone; that we are here to continue their journeys, to keep carrying the flame as they did and one day to pass it on to the next generation. Whenever we feel alone and afraid, she told me, we must stand tall in the knowledge that we have a legion of wise souls standing with us. We should try to move through life with courage and humility and never forget that our journey is one of service.

Mme Ouédraogo was Minister of Social Affairs in the government of the legendary Burkina Faso revolutionary and president, Thomas Sankara. From her I learned of his dream to "reinvent the future" of Africa. Before he could complete his mission, he and twelve of his cabinet ministers were killed in 1987 in an attack, it is said, on the orders of his best friend and second-in-command, Blaise Compaoré. Sankara was an activist for social justice who stood for equality, human rights and especially for women's rights.

Mme Ouédraogo told me that whenever a minister presented a policy, Sankara would send them to the market to explain it to the women who ran stalls there. If the women did not understand it, the minister had to re-write the policy until it was in language that they could understand. Sankara saw himself as a servant of the people, he lived simply, drove an ordinary car and drew a relatively low salary he, himself, had capped. This was while many of his contemporaries had begun enriching themselves on public funds and some saw him as a threat.

When I visited Ouagadougou, the capital of Burkina Faso in 2017 Mme Ouedraogo had just been nominated as Minister of Justice. At lunch she told me that her first assignment had been to exhume the mass grave of Sankara and his colleagues. The official death certificate thirty years before had declared that he had died of "natural causes" but after his body was exhumed, it was found that all the bullets were lodged in his rib cage. He had had his hands up in surrender when he was murdered. We continued our lunch mostly in silent acknowledgement that the work continues, and the struggle goes on. 'It's interesting how life comes full circle thirty years later', she told me. 'Here I am as Minister of Justice, and the first order of the day is to exhume the mass grave of my president, Sankara and my colleagues. I could have been in that grave with them had I not had another meeting to attend that day.'

What emerged from my discussions with all these leaders was extraordinary both in its power and in its simplicity. They each approached leadership in a similar way and I was stunned to recognise that their views represented exactly how my grandmother, Almazesha, my first and number one leader, had always behaved. The matriarch of our family, a widely respected community leader, had fed me leadership lessons along with bedtime stories and tales of the family and her hopes for the future.

What each of these elders had shown me was that their leadership was built on a foundation of humility and dignity. Each of them was patient with others, a great listener, able to give space to others to air their views before responding. They treated people fairly and vowed to never humiliate anyone; they were slow to reprimand and remained present. Each of these principles was underscored by kindness and compassion – values that are even more needed in these times. And all of it was wrapped up in a healthy layer of optimism.

IV

DIGNITY

Good leaders are humble. They are confident in themselves and in their abilities and, at the same time, they are aware of their own limitations. They are open to criticism and see themselves as continuously learning. They take responsibility for their actions and they admit their errors; they are patient with others; grateful for what they have and are at peace with themselves. Good leaders are slow to offend and quick to forgive and they have a healthy, and often self-deprecating, sense of humour. They see others as having inherent dignity; and they acknowledge their worth and treat them with respect. They give them their full attention and really listen to them when they speak. They understand that it's only a combination of chance, hard work and being in the right place at the right time that has earned them their positions.

My grandmother used to always tell us children that each one of us is a creation of God and as such, we must respect and uphold the dignity of every other person. 'Everyone is someone's child. Be kind to them', she would always say. 'No matter who is in front of you, treat them with dignity and respect, with kindness.'

She would often fetch my sisters and I from school and wait for us in the front passenger seat of her olive green Fiat 125 with her driver, Abdel Aziz behind the wheel. Our ritual was that as we climbed on to the brown leather seats of "Fiatwa" – the feminine nickname we gave to the car – a group of street vendors would come running up to us with a range of mouth-watering wares on offer neatly laid out in home-made cardboard display boxes strapped to their shoulders. A few regulars would usually rush up to Fiatwa, as my grandmother was known to be a big spender.

Shiny packs of Wrigley's chewing gum, a pack for twenty-five cents, we called "seemoony" or one piece of gum for five cents, "amist çantim" tempted us from one of the shelves; on another, bubble gum complete with a tattoo transfer of Scooby Doo, Tom and Jerry or Tweety Bird which you could lick and stick to your skin. If you opted for peanuts they would be handed over in a neatly folded little cone made of old newspapers and, for the more studious types, there were pens and pencils, sharpeners and erasers. We would usually each get a candy or sugar-coated nuts or a lollipop after Almazesha had handed over the coins to the eager young salesman. I was puzzled when Abdel Aziz also got a candy because he was a large grown man. My grandmother always seemed to catch my expression in the rear view mirror and she would look back at me and explain softly, 'He is also his mother's child.'

Much later on in my life, I understood what she meant. She was demonstrating that she saw and honoured the humanity in everyone and she wanted us to see that she treated each person with her full attention and kindness, irrespective of their social standing. This is what a good leader does, they recognise that everyone matters and they show this by upholding their dignity.

I had just launched my first NGO in 2003, with a team of sixty-two vibrant and energetic young people. Our goal was to work on leadership and economic development as a strategic approach to help overcome the spread of HIV/AIDS in the community. I asked a small group at the office to create a team page on our website and to include a headshot of every team member with a short inspirational message from each of them.

When it was all done, I saw that Mehdi did not appear on the website. He was the shoeshine guy who worked at the entrance of our building. I always talked to him when I arrived in the morning or when I was on my break. I once mentioned to him that I could not find someone to clean our office; and he generously offered to help me out. So, from early on, Mehdi was the first person in the office with me when I opened up every day at seven a.m. As I prepared in silence for my day, he would move around the office, humming as he cleaned, polishing the hardwood floor and emptying dustbins. We spoke very little but felt connected.

I asked the small team of IT guys why Medhi was not on the website. 'Mehdi the cleaner?' they asked. 'He is just a cleaner.' My heart sank. Mehdi was certainly 'just a cleaner' for many; but for me, he was an essential member of the team who made sure that we would enjoy a clean and fresh office every day and he would run downstairs to fetch us macchiatos and lattes whenever we asked. He was a hard-working young man but because he did not have a college degree or a desk job, the others had not considered him as part of the team. This changed immediately after our chat, and Mehdi's picture and his words of wisdom were uploaded to the website along with those of the rest of the team. This story has remained with me because it shows how we tend to hand out the right to dignity to others based on our perception of whether or not they are worth it. It's a good exercise to regularly look at what you do and to examine whether it is inclusive, fair and kind – and rectify it when it is not.

Your leadership is marked by the way you integrate dignity into your behaviour. Observe how you relate to your teammates and colleagues, remember that dignity is nothing that you say or do; rather it is the silent acknowledgement of your humanity and that of theirs. To be able to recognise and honour the dignity of anyone we encounter, we must start with ourselves. We cannot respect others if we do not respect ourselves. All of us, at least once in our lives, have felt we are not good enough. Taking that first step towards recognising your own value is to accept that you are good enough, that you are valuable and that you have the potential to be your best. Accept yourself just the way you are.

As I was growing up, my grandmother would often talk with me of the future and the responsibility we have today to create the reality of tomorrow. She spoke as if she could see the future on the horizon and that, for her, tomorrow could literally be the day after today or it could be many years on from now. She spoke about our fathers as Abatochachen, and our mothers as Enatochachen; her way of referring to our ancestors and forebears, reminiscing about the work they had done in their lives and implying that a duty fell on those of us left behind to continue their journeys. She would tell me that the future happens one moment at a time. That is why each moment is precious, and why we have to be conscious of everything we do or say — because it is what we do with each of our moments that defines our tomorrows.

Almazesha instilled in me that whatever we do in our life, we must do it in the knowledge that we are only here temporarily. When we do that, then the quality of our contribution might emerge as truly in line with the needs and opportunities on the ground. She wanted me to understand that each one of us is a unique and divine being on the one hand and, at the same time, a tiny component of the big picture. Once I acknowledged that, I felt that there could be no obstacle for me to be able to shine in my own way. Through it all, I could not become intoxicated with myself if what I do is from a place of humility and in service to humanity.

Keep reminding yourself that whatever you do you are only a channel, a servant for the greater good. Be grateful that you are able to contribute in your own way, be it in a small or a big way, to help the whole system function better. Tomorrow we will be gone and the best that each of us can hope for is that the good we have done in the world will outshine the bad. We should take nothing for granted and know that it is what we do now, in each moment, that counts the most.

My leaving Africa was, and always will be, the defining moment of my life; a major turning point that has shaped the person I am today. I left Shola, our sefer – our neighbourhood in Addis Ababa, not knowing where we were headed. When we arrived on the other side, in Europe, I began to discover the concept of being a foreigner in a land where Africans were not always accepted.

Despite the fact that dignity is an inalienable right, there are those who sincerely believe that some of us are not worthy of being treated with dignity. I learned that you can't offer dignity if you have not been raised with it. When someone considers you unworthy of dignity, they withdraw it and you ache at the realisation that, to them, you are nothing but someone alien to that environment. You feel it more acutely when you have to show up to register in government halls or offices and when your name is called out, it is so mangled that it tells you this is obviously not your place.

You will always encounter toxic people who bring down your energy more than they make you feel good. There is no escaping them. Unfortunately people don't come with a health warning stuck on their foreheads so we can't know in advance who to avoid. It's only when you have learned the hard way, and how dangerous to your health some people may be, that you can decide to walk away. The key is to know when it is the right time to leave and give yourself the courage to do so. You might feel that you can't walk away, but remember that you do have the option. Even if you can't physically remove yourself, you can guard yourself energetically from people's toxicity. Shield yourself by reinforcing your presence and being compassionate with yourself.

Think of people like Nelson Mandela and Ahmed Kathrada; when they were sentenced to life imprisonment in 1964, a life sentence for political prisoners meant life; they were supposed to die in prison. They and their comrades did not know if they were going to get out alive, but they persevered, every day. They remained strong and they worked and planned and discussed and continued pursuing their dreams and visions, staying true to their purpose.

Today they remain symbols of hope for all of us. Just as they did, remember that you too can survive; you will always have a way out of a difficult situation, even if it is just in your mind. So see toxic people and situations as a gift to reinforce your boundaries, to help clarify your choices and to remind you why you do what you do. Whether you encounter such people in your personal or in your work life, remember they are there to help you to build resilience, and to encourage you to keep on your path. You will learn strategies to deal with them while retaining your humanity and you will be the winner in the end.

Many years after that life-changing morning when I arrived with my family in Brussels after an exhausting and emotionally draining flight from Addis Ababa, it seems at times as if we're still struggling; still just ticking over, although none of us will admit how tired we are. No one says it's time to go home for good, that it's time to right the wrongs and to adjust the clock.

A world away from Addis Ababa, at my new primary school in Brussels, I soon found out how difficult it was to keep holding onto my confidence. When I noticed that some people decided I was not worthy was the moment I first realised my "otherness". I remember feeling from deep in my soul that I no longer belonged. Gone was the familiar feeling of being welcomed and loved. Back in the seventies, very few of the other students had even heard of a country called Ethiopia. All they knew of Africa was Congo, the former Belgian colony then called Zaire. 'Tu viens d'Afrique', they would boldly announce, declaring that I must come from Africa because I am black. That was not always enough for them; they sought out more precise stereotypical descriptions, throwing learned racist references into the mix. 'Zairoise?' My black skin told them that I must be from Zaire. The fact that it was a lighter shade had them enquiring, 'Métisse?' Perhaps my father was a white Belgian and my mother was Zairoise? They needed me to fit into their boxes.

One day in class Bruno, one of the popular guys in the school, gave us a presentation about racism. I was the only black student in that class. Actually my sisters and I were the only black students in the whole school and in the entire neighbourhood. Racism? I had no clue what Bruno was talking about. I had never heard of it. At the end of his talk, our lanky teacher with scruffy blond hair, Mr. Rosseyls, asked me to share my experience of racism. I thought it might be a taboo political ideology like communism, socialism or imperialism. I had been well trained in the few months of the Derg times, not to talk about politics – I had been taught at home that if you do, you could wind up either being locked up, tortured or killed. So I told him I would rather not comment. He must have assumed my unwillingness to talk came from a profound statement about racism because he didn't insist. I was just relieved that the questioning stopped.

For a moment, I wondered if this country of foreigners had also experienced the trauma of a coup, like mine had – although I had not yet seen armed soldiers or heard machine gun fire in Brussels. My classmates and others in the school saw my sisters and I as the newly arrived Africans with no name, no story and no culture. We wondered how long we would have to stay in Belgium before finally being able to go home.

It took years and in that time I learned much more about racism, about what it means to emigrate and how, once we land in another person's country, we lose our right to demand equal treatment, let alone dignity. It is like being a guest in someone's home and expecting to be accepted as a fully-fledged member of the family. It is not possible to make such a demand; it is up to the host to decide how to treat a guest, is it not?

Racism took on a whole new meaning for me then. I can't say I experienced it directly, but there was a lot of covert racism. Every day subtle racism slowly gnawed away at my self-esteem. My sisters and I were treated like numbers, random individuals without a story, without roots or a place where we belonged. It kept creeping up closer – in the way people looked at you, letting you know that to them you are nothing more than a figure, a label, an object. You have no story, no soul and no spirit. You don't get any of the warmth or the human recognition that you see others being given. Layers of micro-aggressions left me feeling like a ghost, present but invisible, not counted. Unworthy.

I would often think that while our neighbours, our schoolmates and our teachers didn't know where we really came from, or know our stories, there was a place somewhere in the world where people knew me and our family's history, where we fitted in. But in Brussels we were to be judged by the reality of people who were not even curious to get to know us, slamming shut the space for mutual discovery.

I told myself that one day I would go back and help my country become one that people would not want to leave. Until then I would have to work hard to be the best I could be. Once you have left the land of your birth, you may never go back and if you do return you won't be able to fit in exactly as you once did; you find that you have changed as a person just as much as your homeland has.

It happened to me. I did return to Ethiopia, nearly twenty-five years after we left, and worked there for a time, but it was not the same. To this day the hunger for the home I once knew still haunts me and I have come to accept it as part of my being.

I now know that my home is in my heart and it travels with me. Everyone has a place within them; where memories of both happiness and misery have settled into their souls. However naïve this may sound I still maintain that people should have the right to belong wherever in the world they choose. My heart home is Ethiopia, where I was born, where my spirit is at rest; but my true home is the world with all the friends and memories I have made throughout my life. I refuse to accept that I am not a welcome guest wherever I choose to live.

V

PATIENCE

Humans are reactive by default, so in conversation, instead of listening attentively, we are mostly already preparing our answer while the other person is talking. Often we don't even understand what they are saying because we think we already know what they have to say. Good leaders are patient. They give the gift of listening so that they can respond with quality.

Always listen with your heart, let the message land. Take a few breaths to process what you have heard and if there is any doubt, get it clarified. Take a moment to recall the reason for the conversation, remember your own purpose and role, your own values and then and only then, respond.

Let's say a colleague gives you feedback, whether it is genuine or not, listen and take in all they say. Check with yourself if what they have said makes sense to you. Suspend judgement and listen; don't make it personal, it's just feedback. Don't get offended. Remember that everyone has their own perspective and the feedback will either help you expand your perspective or help them expand theirs. Take it as an opportunity to learn something.

If there is a tone of conflict, absorb what is being said, and either engage with it, find a way to compromise or stand courageously in defence of your position. When you engage, use clear and precise language. Say what you mean and mean what you say in ways that are as respectful and as authentic as possible. Remember that conflict only arises when what we want is different from what the other person wants. The only constructive way out of conflict is dialogue and conversation. This doesn't just mean talking but also listening carefully to fully understand.

We cannot lead well if we are not prepared to listen. Whether it means listening to what our own hearts say or what other people are saying, we need to take care to listen with quality. It is tempting in our fast-paced lives, to make decisions quickly, and to urge others to cut to the chase. If anything, what I have learned from the leaders I spent time with, was that exercising patience is essential. Listening is a skill of patience and focus that helps us to give dignity to others. Hear them out until they are done.

Just as most of us are guilty of already having prepared a reply while another person is still speaking, the same happens when we want to be heard and we can tell that the other person is looking for a gap to jump in. If we want support from others and if we want them to hear us and to really understand what we are saying, they must be able to expect and receive our full attention. In the same way, if we are asking someone to listen to us, it's only respectful for them to give us their attention.

When we are in conversation with another person, the quality of that exchange is directly related to the attention we give each other. When we listen deeply and with authenticity, we trigger a much higher level of thinking, allowing a richer exchange. If you want to listen deeply you must be 90 per cent silent and talk for only 10 per cent of the time. It's simple, the more you are silent, the more you can focus on the message and the more chance you will have to actually understand what is being communicated. Listening is a gift. The more you listen with quality and intent to understand what is being said, the more you will honour the person talking to you.

What struck me when I sat with the elders, was that the greater the leader was, the more they said they would always first listen carefully to what other people had to say before offering their own point of view. They had no urge to speak unless they felt they had something significant to say. When they did eventually speak, what they said was often so crisp, clear and uncluttered precisely because they said what they meant and they meant what they said, and they said it with respect. They listened before they responded to allow themselves the space to really hear and understand what was being said to them, not just to answer. They spoke to complement the conversation and to gear themselves towards helping to find a solution; to offer a contribution without having their views dominate the discussion. They spoke only if they believed that what they wanted to say would add value to what has already been put on the table.

Isn't that a refreshing change? How many of us listen with half an ear to someone? We wait for a gap in the narrative so we can dive in with our reaction, to slam down our own views before the person has finished what they had set out to say. And how many of us know what it feels like when we become aware that the person we are talking to is just not listening? I am sure you know how it is to be in a meeting when someone's attention begins to wander and it is your turn to speak. There's always that person who looks away from you, gets busy with their diary or other notes. And then, when their turn comes, they miraculously bring their attention back into the room. As a consequence some of us find that we have learned to speak more quickly and more loudly in meetings because we are interrupted and spoken over so often that we expect it to happen. So we subconsciously set up barriers to it. Doesn't it feel at times as if you are merely part of an audience listening to a series of speeches and monologues? It can be exhausting and it can leave you feeling unseen, unconsidered and unworthy. This is not the mark of good leadership.

If we don't listen to what someone is saying how can we ever know what their reality is, how they might want to change it or even how they might be able to contribute towards a solid team innovation? By not listening carefully we will never really find out what their dreams are and we will never be able to properly help another person to achieve their vision.

When you are a real listener you will be patient, slow to speak and you will open yourself up more to others; you will, in turn, encourage them to open up to you too. When you do begin to speak, it will be in such a way as to allow others to overcome their doubts and their limitations and any biases they may have. When you show them what you see as a solution, it will be done in such a respectful way that they will want to go there with you, to follow you and make your dream theirs too. When you show them that they matter to you, they will be more likely to want to follow you.

Leaders who are game changers have the ability to relate to others and, through those relationships, they create the space for others to consider a different reality, another outcome. Dare to also listen to yourself, to be quiet in order to hear what your own heart is trying to tell you and then have the courage to do what it suggests.

No change is comfortable because for change to happen it usually means we have to alter our routine, to modify some of the certainty we have grown comfortable with or change some of the habits we are used to. Most of us have some level of insecurity about doing this; but be ready to be uncomfortable, to be challenged, the more you are able to do that, the more you will be able to realise positive change in your life.

Sometimes the habits you must change come from deep-seated cultural norms. Each of us is located within a society, a community and a social class, which operates according to certain strictures, and they tell us what we should do and what we should not do. We all know how our own world works, what society discourages and what it welcomes and to what extent we are prepared to defy. In my country of birth, Ethiopia, it is frowned upon to disagree with older people. Does that make me a rude person when I do disagree? Or do I work within these restrictions and find ways to do it without causing offence? It can be complicated when you are in a work environment where you need to disagree with a policy, an action or a person. We find ourselves looking at this life "outside" of our community's standards and having to decide whether to keep or discard a pattern of behaviour.

Give yourself permission to do things differently. Give yourself permission not to comply. Allow yourself to be yourself.

Sit with it and see if you can learn to be at peace with doing something you were always taught is not acceptable to do. This will help you to expand yourself. I'm not a saint, I don't want to be nice with everybody and that's okay too. So the more I give myself permission to disagree and to stand up for myself, the more I stand in integrity to my humanity, and my inner self, and the stronger I will become. Don't sabotage yourself by holding back and behaving in a way that you know won't work.

I was also brought up to believe that crying, showing weakness or being indecisive was not acceptable. I was raised to control and suppress my emotions. So I learned to keep quiet about whatever might be causing me to feel sad. We had to be strong and soldier on. It took me a long time to be able to sit with the discomfort overtly feminine women brought to me. They represented everything I was told not to be. Later, I had to work to reclaim my feminine side and bring it back into the light. It was not an easy journey but the result left me feeling complete, of being okay with myself and with others, no matter how they choose to show up. I am now at ease with my feminine side, I own it.

I have reached the point where I can accept that I am perfect in my imperfection and that I can decide to stop listening to people who try to make me conform to their measures of approval. There will always be someone who wants you to change; sometimes the change is for your own good; and sometimes it's just to comply with accepted norms. The way to know the difference is to suspend judgement towards yourself. Be your own best friend first, be kind to yourself, have compassion for yourself and have gratitude for your life. If you are comfortable with who you are, then you can certainly be your own best friend. Try it; you will be surprised how it will impact your life. When you are your own best friend first, then you will have the power to be a good friend to others.

When you give yourself permission to accept the blessings of life, it will allow you to be grateful. Once you have a sense of gratitude for who you are and what you have, you can be grateful for others and this can open you up to other opportunities you might not have noticed otherwise.

VI

THE POWER OF CHOICE

We all have choice and choice is power. When we know what we want to change or what needs to change, the next step is to figure out how to do it. We must train ourselves to listen to our inner voice and to also pay attention to what others are saying. Change starts the minute you make a choice.

Our ability to exercise choice is impacted either negatively or positively by the contexts in which we live; and it is constrained by cultural norms. We always have the choice to change how we behave, how we are going to act and react. This is particularly useful in stressful situations. Between the moment that something happens and the moment that we react to it, there is a slither of time, a golden opportunity to choose, to be intentional about how we can helpfully respond. We can start each day by choosing how we are going to show up in the world, how we are going to be with other people, and most importantly, how we will react when the unexpected happens.

My parents chose to leave Ethiopia. They decided, like thousands of others that we, as a family, must leave to survive. Their dream was just to find us a place where we could live in peace and safety. The anxiety over Covid-19 has many similarities to how we felt when we fled Ethiopia. You just don't know what the next moment will bring; there is absolutely no guarantee that things will be okay again; and no one seems to have the answers you seek. We just need to keep motivated to make the little changes that we can to keep pursuing our dreams and our visions.

In my own life, change is often preceded by the feeling that my world has shrunk; it suddenly feels oddly tight and uncomfortable in places and I am moved to do something to correct it. Sometimes radical change happens when we are fed up with a situation and some inner inspiration and strength pushes us to manifest incredible change. A chain-smoker may just drop the habit one day. When people can no longer tolerate injustice, when social balance is lost and reality is skewed, the collective can find the spark to rise up and create a new order.

Whether we want to change our own lives or those of our families, whether we want to change a community or a nation, the process is the same. Experiencing that feeling of discomfort is what allows any of us to make an effort to change, to transform our reality.

The next step is knowing to "what" I want to change. Whatever the reason, it is up to me to figure it out, and then to find a solution. The same process can apply to larger-scale, more complex change because many more people and institutions are involved.

The seed or spark of change emerges with the discomfort of our current reality, its tightness or pain. We move towards change when not taking action is more painful than the burden of embarking on change. The challenge and the reason why most efforts at change fail is that most of us don't make it through the transition phase – the gap between the current and the desired state.

I often think about the power of choice in the lives of those who were incarcerated like many of my relatives who were political prisoners. They made the choice to establish a routine of daily physical exercise, to work out every day in the tiny, cold, concrete boxes in which they were forced to live. They chose to do sit-ups, push-ups and running on the spot. They chose to put their physical and mental health into their own hands. They chose to react with dignity when they were abused by prison guards and they chose not to fall apart when they received bad news from outside. They accepted that while their bodies were not free, their minds were and their jailers could not control their thoughts.

I did not interview Nelson Mandela about his style of leadership, but I am confident that the characteristics of his leadership are similar to the basic principles Mr K and the other leaders shared with me. In an encouraging letter from Robben Island prison to his jailed wife, Winnie Mandela in 1975, Mandela may as well have been outlining what he believed to be the essence of a good leader when he wrote:

> *In judging our progress as individuals we tend to concentrate on external factors such as one's social position, influence and popularity, wealth and standard of education. These are, of course, important in measuring one's success in material matters and it is perfectly understandable if many people exert themselves mainly to achieve all these. But internal factors may be even more crucial in assessing our development as a human being. Honesty, sincerity, simplicity, humility, pure generosity, absence of vanity, readiness to serve others – qualities which are within easy reach of every soul – are the foundation of one's spiritual life.*

While most of us will not go through the experience of long-term imprisonment, how Mandela, Mr K and their comrades behaved in prison is a very good example of the power of choice in our lives and how, no matter the obstacles we face, we are able to keep ourselves balanced. All the little choices we make every day may not seem so significant at the time but if we get into the habit of consciously making the right choices, we will be able to look back and see the difference they made.

I once knew a woman whose choices changed her life completely. Let's call her Rose. She was employed as a housekeeper and was hardworking and punctual, she showed up early for work, started on time and didn't take off her apron until it was time to go home. She was religiously and surgically precise about what she did and, above all, she was kind. One day, she found out that she was pregnant, again. She couldn't afford another child and was considering having an abortion. She took on board all the views offered by everyone she had consulted and eventually decided that she would seek better paying work to help handle the extra costs of another baby. We helped her to find another job, not in a private house but in an office. She did well, earned better and was helping to provide for her growing family.

Later she found out that her husband had been spending her hard-earned money on other women. They divorced and she and her newborn baby and her college student daughter had to leave the family home. All they could find was one room in a compound with no bathroom, and they had to share one mattress. Slowly Rose's hard work began to be noticed at her place of employment. She was promoted to the position of messenger and when the receptionist resigned, her employers urged her to take the job. She almost convinced herself she could not do it, but she did. She went higher and higher within the same company until she became part of the top team managing various projects and reporting directly to the country director of the organisation.

Rose attributed her success mainly to having made the right choices to improve her life and that of her children. These choices had opened the way to her transformation. She shows us how changing one life at a time can be so powerful and reminds us of our potential to create change both in our own lives and in the lives of others.

In the early 2000s, we started a community radio programme to support our work on the prevention of HIV/AIDS. It aired every Saturday morning for ninety minutes on FANA radio, then the largest government radio station in Ethiopia. We would collect stories at the community level during the week and choose one we would air. One Saturday we featured the story of a secretary who needed her boss' permission to attend a training course abroad. When she raised it with him, he told her he would only allow her to go if she had sex with him. She was married, and was committed to her family and her husband. She refused the offer and the overseas trip was no longer possible.

After some time her boss asked her to stay late at work. That evening, after everyone else had gone home, he assaulted and raped her. She chose not to tell her husband for fear of his reaction, and she decided not to have intimate relations with him until she found out what her HIV status was. He became suspicious and, thinking that she might be having an affair, he started beating her up. She faced an unbearable dilemma: If she told him about the rape, he might not believe her; and if she told the authorities about the rape, she would end up carrying the shame.

We told her story in a nationwide broadcast accessible to around forty million listeners. We called her Sarah and opened the phone lines at various points of her narrative to encourage listeners to call in and to speak as if they were her. Men, women, younger and older listeners called in and said things like, 'Hello, this is Sarah. I am afraid and I don't know where to turn. What will happen to my children, how can my husband suspect me of having an affair?' This allowed the audience to reflect on and discuss these issues as if they were their own. It gave them the chance to look into themselves and their responses while, at the same time, empowering them to make informed choices about their own challenges.

The show gave the listeners an opportunity to revisit their own values and to see how they were aligned with how they behaved in the world. We also looked at how our conservative culture dictated the way we should behave. Many listeners called in, wondering where they could report rape without feeling ashamed, where they could go for treatment, therapy and even justice. Many other issues were raised, and each one pointed to a different aspect of society, our personal values and those of our culture.

Around the same time I met a man called Abraham who had contracted polio and leprosy at the age of six. By the time he was eight he had to leave his village in the north of Ethiopia to go to the capital, Addis Ababa, and join the hundreds of mostly physically disabled beggars. He had lost most of his fingers, and his face had become quite scarred and because he had had polio, he could not walk properly. He moved around with the help of a sad version of a skateboard made from a discarded piece of board. He lived in the gutters and sometimes in the cavernous sewerage system below the streets and mostly only came out at night to beg or to look for food. Before heading back to the gutter before dawn, he would stop at the local bars and either buy Tej, the local honey wine, or collect enough of the last bits left from each customer's leftovers to create a glass for himself. And then he would disappear back under the city.

When things got really bad, Abraham went to the hospital to seek treatment. The standard option then was to amputate the sufferer's legs but, for some reason this time, the doctor refused and opted instead for a surgical option. After a series of operations, and many years of treatment, Abraham still had both legs, walked straight up, and had also been treated to stop the disease progressing. By the time I met him, a few years after his surgery, he had left the gutters and lived in a plastic house. This was an upgrade. He was not a beggar anymore; he had joined a church and started serving its community as a member of its prayer team.

I was going through my own set of challenges, and he soon became my spiritual teacher. When I left the office, at lunchtime or after work, I would sometimes go and sit with Abraham in the neighbourhood where others affected by leprosy lived. In the beginning, the residents couldn't understand what I was doing there, because the area was almost completely closed off from anyone who did not have leprosy.

Being with Abraham and his community gave me a chance to breathe and rest. It gave me time to introspect and pray. His prayers were powerful, and his guidance helped me deal with my work in the office and with my private life. Eventually, my visits to him became so normal and regular that his friends would notice if I had not come by. They would often ask me if all was well with me and asked why I had not come to visit.

When I established my own organisation, I hired Abraham as a community worker, and made him responsible for the people in the community who lived with leprosy. I tried to meet weekly with all team members to catch up on what had happened that week, what to expect for the following week, and how all of it fitted into the greater plan of the organisation.

At one meeting a miracle happened after I told everyone that if they missed submitting their weekly reports twice in row they would be fired. Abraham raised his hands to show that he had no fingers and couldn't write. Using my nickname he said, 'Mimi, that's not fair, how should I manage this?' he asked, waving his hands pleadingly. 'However you decide; it's your decision, and not mine', I replied sharply. 'There will be no exception, you will be fired if you miss submitting your weekly report on time.' I said it, not because I did not empathise with him, but because the reply just came blurting out of my mouth. I was shocked at myself for being so unsympathetic, but later realised that my answer had come from a deep place in my heart; a place that stood for Abraham and his potential; a place where I felt that discrimination was disempowering. I wanted to see him emerge from his circumstances and continue to make his own choices, to be able to work himself free of his physical limitations.

The entire team was appalled that I could lose my manners like that. They all stared at me, and then back at Abraham. A second later, his energy changed until the biggest smile was plastered across his face. My stand had given him the green light to go; it gave him the recognition that, despite his disabilities, he had as many opportunities as anyone else had. Even though throughout his life, he had been considered to be useless and hopeless, that day he knew it was not true. What was true was that he could take on his physical challenges and overcome them to access the kind of life he wanted.

I believe that, in the end, Abraham found someone to work with him to write his reports; he would dictate and the other person would note down what he said. He became so motivated, and would walk miles from his home to our office and back carrying an empty laptop bag, slightly tilting his body to reflect the weight of the imaginary machine. 'One day, you'll find that I am the owner of a real laptop', he vowed with a mischievous grin.

These are not just the good luck stories of a couple of individuals. Wherever I go I am reminded of the power we all have to become change agents, when we give ourselves permission to make choices about our lives. Rose is going from strength to strength in her career, Sarah is raising her family and continuing her work as an HIV/AIDS activist, and Abraham has built a brick house, has got married and is the father of two healthy daughters. Their choices brought great change to their lives and they are now helping to transform the lives of others.

VII

PRESENCE

Have you ever been in the middle of a conversation and you realise you cannot remember what the person talking to you had just said? It is because you did not listen, you were not present.

Being present, or being mindful, is an intentional act. We have to train our minds to do it and we must practise it and keep on practising it. We must choose to be present. We don't realise the moment we fall out of being present. It is only when we awake from being absent do we realise we were not fully there.

I think that one of the main reasons we stop being present is our tendency to multitask. Instead of focusing on one thing and doing just that until we finish, we think we can cheat time by doing several things at once. Unfortunately, our brain is not configured to do that perfectly. It can only do one thing at a time, to do it well. When we multitask, we do a less than good job of all the things we are trying to do at the same time. We will make mistakes, and we will have to come back to correct things we've done not so well and we will forget things.

To train yourself to be present, focus on what it is you really want to do. Allocate yourself an attention budget. What amount of attention do you want to give to each of the things you have to do? Each one of us only has twenty-four hours a day, of which we need to sleep and be with our families for about ten hours of the twenty-four. If you take another three hours out to shower, dress, prepare meals and eat, that only leaves you with eleven hours. Decide on what, realistically, you can achieve in those eleven hours. Then break that down; allocate yourself the time you need for all your other tasks, it will help you focus better and you will end up achieving more. Keep in mind that to be present means that you are living wholeheartedly, living with awareness. When we are not present it is as if we are living absent-mindedly. If we did the calculations we would see that most of us spend hardly any time living mindfully.

When the leaders I interviewed spoke about their secret to leading well, I became aware that, although they didn't use this terminology themselves, what they essentially all described as part of their style was mindfulness. They were all way ahead of their time, some of them practising being present decades before the Buddhist monk Thich Nhat Hanh started to teach it in the mid-1970s.

Mindfulness is about being present, giving all your attention to what is said and done around you;

it is about being aware of your actions and how they impact on others and also on yourself. You could say it is like putting everything into slow motion and observing it as it unfolds. Because it is slow you can carefully consider what to say and how to say it before you open your mouth. This way of being is in harmony with what the leaders expressed when they said they listened before they spoke, were slow to react and took care not to humiliate others. Being present in this way gives you the space to think about the consequences of reacting before you react. It gives you better control in many tricky situations and allows you to retain your own dignity and, to an extent, the dignity of all those you encounter.

Decide to remain mindful every day of what is around you and what is in your thoughts. And remember that the journey towards your vision is not a straight line, it's a process. Mindfulness can also help you to make sense of the inner chatter, the commentary buzzing in your head all day long about everything that you see and feel. When this voice is just humming in the background, it's nothing but a jumble of ramblings in your head. But when it gets louder and starts commenting, this is what leads us to judgement, to make assumptions. And this is normal. When we are present and aware of it and how we react, we will be able to suspend judgement and hold back from making assumptions. It is this that will help us to be fair with others. Fairness creates space for trust and the building of better relationships, which, in turn, creates more understanding. One way to ensure fairness is to make sure to stay as objective as possible, to listen to all that is said and also to what is unsaid and take time to make decisions.

When you are present you will also be in a better position to carry out your own dreams and visions. Think of where you want to see yourself in a year from now. Note the date; decide where you want to be; who you want to be; and how you want to be showing up in the world. You might want to take the exercise further and imagine what it will be like for you in another five years; what will you look like; what will you be doing in the world; who will your friends be? Mark the date and make some notes: where do you want to be; what kind of individual do you want to be; what life and work habits would you have increased? What habits would you have let go of? Every day visualise the person you are going to become and imagine how your life would have transformed.

The future is there on the horizon, it will happen however it happens, but our choices will help to fashion what it will look like. If we do nothing about helping to sculpt this future, it will happen without us. But train yourself to be there and to be present and you can have more control over how it turns out. If you decide, for instance, that in five years you are going to be happy, and at your peak physically, emotionally and mentally, and supported by friends and colleagues, think of what choices you will need to make today for this to happen. You might decide to mute the people who sabotage your plans by draining your energy. You might decide that whatever they say or do you are not going to let them affect you. On the contrary, you might decide to turn up the volume on people who make you feel good.

Think of the habits you already have that can propel you forward to that vision. Which patterns do you need to let go of to get onto a path to fulfill your vision? Remember to always shift any negative thoughts. You might have got up in the morning, thought you look like hell and began to feel bad about yourself. Why don't you give yourself some kindness and compassion? 'Hey friend, you look like you need some rest. Or, okay, don't scare people now. Let's find something good to wear.'

My grandmother, Almazesha was my first leader, and as I sought to understand what guided her I was always led to what I believe are the essential components of good leadership. She remained the same person through the time of the Emperor, the time of the communist regime and to her last days in our democracy. She lived through times of peace and also through times of war. She experienced family tragedies, sorrow and happiness. She lived through economic downturns as well as growth. The philosopher Friedrich Nietzsche is widely quoted to have said, 'If you know the why, you can live anyhow.' I believe Almazesha was clear about the "why" of her life. It was to be of service and that is what made it so easy for her to live her life. Being clear about why we do what we do, and anchoring ourselves in a cause that is much greater than ourselves is essential if we are to live effectively.

Do you remember a time when you were so engaged in something you absolutely believed in that you would jump out of bed to write down your ideas? You would work endlessly because you did not see the time pass; you were in such a flow. Well it happened because whatever you were doing was precisely aligned with your inner values. You were simply being yourself and that is why it was easy to flow. Everything unfolds naturally when you are in flow. It's no effort, it simply is.

Part of being present is to also take time out for reflection every day. We all feel overwhelmed by life at times. The bills, the chores, the family, the job, the pandemic and all sorts of concerns about the future tend to build up until they leave us feeling demoralised and powerless. The trouble is we don't always make the space to give ourselves the chance to revitalise, to recharge our batteries. All of us need that time just to be still, to breathe and to reconnect with ourselves.

I find that making time every day for quiet reflection gives me a break from all the stresses around and within me and it helps to give me greater clarity and energy. By building meditation time into your daily routine you can keep your own battery charged and keep yourself optimistic no matter what else is happening in your world.

Meditation, or just sitting in nature, will help you to go to a place where you can connect with your soul, your greater self; where you feel as if you can tap into your subconscious and connect with who you felt you were before everything seemed too big to deal with. It can help you to resuscitate the essential greatness you may have forgotten you had and the gifts that only you can give to the world. While meditation is a formal mindfulness practise, the fact is that there are an infinite number of informal mindfulness practises. Anything you can do to bring your awareness to the present moment, whether you are doing the dishes, cooking or going to the gym, running or painting, drawing or even driving on a long road – all of it can be a mindfulness practise. It is simply about being a witness to your life, as you live it one moment at a time. This will allow you to live your life with intention.

Instead of reacting automatically, thoughtlessly to all that happens around you, mindfulness allows you to stretch time so that you can be intentional about the choices you make. And this is what will take your leadership to the next level, to another dimension.

Whether you want to try out formal or informal mindfulness practises, commit yourself to every day for two or three weeks and notice how it makes you feel and how it improves the quality of your interactions.

VIII

STAYING THE COURSE

Leadership is not a sprint; it's a marathon and, at times, it can even feel like a triathlon. We have to stay the course no matter what challenges and obstacles come our way. We must become resilient and be persistent; keep our eyes on the horizon, and always connect with our purpose and vision.

There will be encounters that knock our confidence and make us want to give up. How we decide to handle them is crucial. It is easy to attack someone who has wronged us, but we should keep mindful of the repercussions our words can have, give ourselves the chance to slow down, and choose our reactions more carefully.

When I first tried to move back to Ethiopia in the late 1980s, my friends wondered what in the world was wrong with me. How could I leave the life I had built in Europe and in the United States and want to go back to Africa? They were not the only ones. I was once stuck in an elevator in Addis Ababa with a government official, a man old enough to be my grandfather. We had time to converse; or rather I had time to respond to his barrage of questions about why on earth I had come back. My answer was sincere – I wanted to be closer to my family and to apply what I had learned in other parts of the world. I wanted to help. He laughed cynically and said something like, 'Yeah, right. You probably dropped out of school or you couldn't manage life out there. That's why you are back. You young people will say anything just to look good. All liars, all a bunch of liars', he snarled. I was stunned. I felt tied by the dictates of my culture not to disrespect an elder and I had to keep quiet until the door opened. His attitude only made me more determined to follow my dreams.

Once you have found your purpose and you have visualised it and invested in it, go for it and keep pursuing it. Decide that you will not compare yourself to others; that you will not be swayed from your vision after every comment, positive or negative. Accept the opinions of others but decide that you will not be threatened by negative reactions or seek validation from others. You know better than anyone what it is that your heart desires. Do your very best and know that this is all you can do.

Make sure that you invest enough time in yourself so that you are very clear about what this vision is going to look like in the long term. So what if people knock your idea? You are doing your bit, making your contribution. Sometimes unconstructive criticism from others is just a reflection of their own vulnerability. Take a deep breath and remind yourself of what you are trying to do to make your own life more meaningful. Ask yourself the question that if you knew you would not be here tomorrow; would you be doing the same thing? Be so convinced about what you are doing that no one will be able to persuade you to give it up.

While it can feel gloomy, I believe it is important to keep the knowledge of our own inevitable death very close to us. It helps to put everything into sharp focus and helps us to achieve our dreams. When we reflect on our values and principles and are intentional about our choices, we can start to live our lives authentically, rather than be influenced by the opinion of others.

This is how we take ownership of what we stand for and how we can build the courage to follow our dreams, no matter what the consequences may be. Remember and recognise that we all have different roles in different contexts. Be clear about your unique role within your context. Give yourself the option to keep learning and keep strengthening your competences. Own your responsibilities and, at the same time, own your weaknesses and strengths. Resolve to keep getting better at what you do; keep re-evaluating where you are and look for room for improvement.

Remember that we are all a work in progress.

I was once in a conversation with an unkind and egocentric person who was draining my energy by not allowing me to contribute to the conversation. I imagined that perhaps he was trying to take up all the space in the room because, for whatever reason, he felt vulnerable. I decided that, to honour both of us, I would let him act out his own issues without confronting him. I said to myself, 'Well done you, you're fine, you're good.' I had refused to accept what his own issues had triggered. There was no way I could get inside his head to see what thoughts were defining his feelings and his actions, but I could examine my own; I could control what I thought and how I acted.

Whatever negative situation we are in, if we first acknowledge what there is to be grateful for, it frees us to be more relaxed and to figure out better ways of dealing with things. In this grateful and optimistic way we can control our thoughts and lay the foundations for how we are able to transform our lives and those of others.

We have all encountered bullying behaviour. Bullies feel they need to take control and to shut others down due to their own fear or insecurity. When we are bullied we feel small, we feel pushed around, we feel unappreciated and humiliated, even insulted. Not all bullying is explicit, it can also be implicit from people we consider to be friends. They have fun at our expense. As long as we let it happen, it will continue. So, it's up to us to stop it. It's up to us to be our own best friends and dare to stand up to it. Take a deep breath and speak your mind. It might be awkward at first; you might lose your words, you might stutter, you might even cry, do it anyway. Next time it happens you will be a little less afraid, a little more courageous. Before you know it, the bullying will decrease and eventually stop.

Each time we stand up to a bully, we give others the right, the strength and the belief that they too can stand up for themselves. Each time we see someone else being bullied, step in and speak to them. Encourage them and support them to stand up to the bully.

Of course, at times, the bully can be our employer, our co-workers or our clients. We have to earn a living, to feed our families, so we fear responding. Don't be afraid, speak up. Being bullied will cost you in terms of your mental health. Sometimes when we are bullied, we subconsciously take it on and pass it on to our loved ones. Be careful of this. Remember that you have the choice to stay in the situation or to step way.

One of the biggest challenges traditionally faced by people committed to creating transformation through positive change was not being able to easily network with like-minded people across the world.

Many people missed out on far-off meetings and workshops because of being unable to raise money or sponsorships to travel. Covid-19 has forced us to accept solutions offered by digital platforms like Zoom and WhatsApp.

Another obstacle to transformation is that it takes time. Be persistent. After the change of government in Ethiopia from the communist regime to the new democratic government in the early 1990s, another conflict was reignited. Eritrea had been fighting for independence from Ethiopia for years, linked to how the Emperor, Haile Selassie, had dealt with the Italian occupation. In 1896, Italian troops tried to colonise Ethiopia but were defeated at the battle of Adwa by Emperor Menelik II. A few decades later, in 1935–1936, the Italians tried again, this time under their dictator, Benito Mussolini, but they were defeated by both the military strategies of our leaders and the endurance and commitment of our soldiers, as well as the fact that our troops were more familiar with our mountainous landscape.

Eventually Italy returned with an array of artillery, beyond what our people could oppose at that time, and managed to occupy Ethiopia for a total of five years. From his exile, the Emperor called on the League of Nations to help free the country from Italian occupation. That resulted in an arrangement that Italy could take the region of Eritrea as a protectorate if they retreated from the rest of the country. After the end of the protectorate, when Italy withdrew from the country, Eritrea wanted to become an independent state. But Ethiopia did not agree, neither under the reinstalled Emperor, Haile Selassie nor under the communist regime. This led to a civil war that lasted close to thirty years.

When our new democratic government took office in 1995, it created a federal state and offered any constituency the choice to become independent. Eritrea could choose to hold an independence referendum or to remain as part of Ethiopia. A falling out between the leaders of Eritrea and Ethiopia led to the two countries deporting citizens from the other and the populations of both countries, some from the same families, were torn apart.

Early one morning in late 1998 on my way home from work, I witnessed desperate scenes of officials removing people from their homes for deportation. Some of my co-workers joked in the office about how cheap it would be to buy goods from the departing Eritreans. My Eritrean colleague, Ephrem, who was born and bred in Ethiopia, was teased by others about when he would be picked up and deported. This wonderful, gentle man who could speak English, French, Italian, Amharic, Tigrigna and some Somali, was taken away a couple of weeks later.

When I heard about this, I could not stop weeping and called Almazesha, my go-to person in good times and in bad. I explained what had happened and she replied simply that if I wanted to help Ephrem, I should stop crying, wash my face and go and find him. Her lesson to me was the importance of remaining calm in a crisis. I immediately went to look for him in the kebele near his house, which had been turned into a detention centre. It was filled with distressed people, so crowded that we had to push our way in. Inside was a heaving mass of people, on the one side, those who were to be deported and on the other, those who were searching for people. All that divided them was a thin line of benches. The line of knee-high flat wooden seats appeared to me then as insurmountable as a towering brick wall.

I finally saw Ephrem and we made eye contact, I felt like crying but I sucked it up, remembering my grandmother's words that I would need to be calm to be able to help him. I took messages from him to his wife, and helped her to arrange the winding down of their lives in Ethiopia before she, too, was deported a few weeks later. We were eventually able to contact each other, through Europe, as mail was not permitted between Ethiopia and Eritrea and one day I connected him with a girlfriend of mine who lived in Asmara.

Through her, I learned that he was well.

These abrupt changes in the life of this one man and all those deported from one country to another, came about as a consequence of a series of choices made through time, each leading to the next. Ephrem saw his whole life turned upside down because of the historical and political changes in Ethiopia where he had spent his entire life. He did not have any real family to speak of in Eritrea. Around the same time, war broke out between our two nations that left bitter wounds on both sides. So many soldiers perished – both Ethiopian and Eritrean; many of them may have been related and would have celebrated somewhere in town together if they had met at a different time, in a different place, with a beer or a cup of coffee at the end of the afternoon.

Kia had worked in the red light district, and was one of the women in our HIV/AIDS prevention programme. She came to me one day asking me to help her find her son. He had been drafted to fight in the Eritrea–Ethiopia conflict. She said she would leave Addis Ababa for the military camps at the frontline to find him and take some Atmit to him; because she was sure he would be unable to get to sleep without first taking this warm, oats-based drink, often prepared for children, convalescents or women who had just given birth. It felt absurd to me when she set off to search for her son to give him a comforting drink, but how could I say that to a mother desperate to help her son, even if he was a soldier heading to war? I could not discourage her, but instead I tried to contribute some money to cover at least the cost of her bus fare. By some miracle she found him and came back to tell us the story. Unlike the one hundred thousand soldiers and citizens who perished in the war, he made it out alive and ended up returning to live with her in Addis Ababa.

These are two examples of how current affairs can impact our day-to-day reality, and how today's policies can define tomorrow's reality and wreak havoc in the lives of ordinary people. Imagine if leaders would incorporate a more humane approach in the way they do politics. Incidentally, Ethiopian Prime Minister Abiy Ahmed Ali, who was a young soldier in the Ethiopia–Eritrea war, won the Nobel Peace Prize in 2019 partly for his initiative to end the conflict.

IX

LEADING WELL

Leadership starts when we embrace our dreams and vision. When we have figured out what our purpose here on earth is and what gifts we have to offer in service of others, then we can start to work on how we lead. Our life's purpose is linked to what makes us happy and gives us meaning. It is what we do simply because it's what we love to do. When we do what we love, it's effortless; and we find pleasure in waking up in the morning to start another day. As we pursue our purpose, we will be able to make the right choices and have the courage to stand up for what we believe in.

We lead well when we lead with our hearts – when we seek to be of service to others, when we embrace change for the benefit of our communities. Let's start with ourselves. Are we comfortable with how we behave in our own circles? Can we do better? Have we placed kindness and compassion for ourselves and for others at the centre of all that we do?

When you lead with your heart you lift the spirit of your team because your team members will notice that the way you relate to them is with authenticity and empathy. Leaders who are game changers have the ability to relate to others by creating the space for them to consider a different reality. The idea that change is impossible becomes 'there might be a way; let's find it'.

No matter what size your organisation is, be it a one-person enterprise or an entity employing hundreds or even thousands of people, ask yourself if you are clear about the horizon you are aiming for and if you have the courage to chase your dreams. Would you be willing to give your team the space and time to innovate and are you willing to be a follower as well as a leader?

Leadership is an expression of what is inside us. What comes out is what is in there already; there is no faking it. Whatever values you hold will emerge in the way you relate to those around you. So it all starts with you, who you are, how you serve your values and what your intention is when you engage with the world. Being true to what we stand for is essential to being able to lead well. Our values are what will help us frame our vision and, at the same time, sustain us on our journey to fulfilling our dreams. The more we align our values with our choices, and our choices with our dreams and vision, the more we will start to flow into our being and life purpose.

It's one thing to know and recognise our values; it's another to adhere to them and put up boundaries when they are not being upheld. It takes courage to speak up when our values are not respected; it sometimes feels so much easier to bury our heads in the sand until the unpleasant feeling goes. Yet, if we are serious about the changes we want to see, we will need to step up when our principles are attacked. It might be that some of us feel that saying "no" might lead us to miss an opportunity. We should learn to say "no" when "no" is needed. Unless we know when to say "no" and have the courage to actually say it, then we must accept that our "yes" will not be as strong as it could be. "Yes" and "No" are essential colours on the palette of life, which help define what we stand for.

As we build our dreams and prepare to work towards them, we should keep in mind that we will meet obstacles along the way. We can surrender to them or we can take them as opportunities to re-invent, re-wire and re-think our path. Don't ever doubt that the obstacles, which very often are human shaped, will do their best to beat our dreams out of us. While we share our dreams with others and can come up with fabulous ideas to implement them, sceptics will discourage us; they will plant seeds of doubt in us because they either can't yet see what we see or they don't want us to succeed for whatever reason.

When we choose to accept these obstacles and challenges as opportunities to re-think, then we will not be dragged down; we will stay on track and be able to constantly remind ourselves of how we will maintain the heartbeat of our dream. Ask yourself, if you choose to keep your dream alive, will you have the courage to walk strongly on the path to realising your potential, even if that means walking alone? If your answer is "yes", how do you plan to do that? What will sustain you through your life's journey?

Your leadership is a permanent work in progress and it will be built as you go along. It will gain scope and depth as you move through and past all the challenges. For every breakdown you encounter, you can create a breakthrough. For every obstacle you face, you have the chance to overcome it and move beyond it. With every opportunity that comes along, you can rise to the challenge.

Check in with yourself regularly. Are you being humble, are you honouring your dignity and that of others; are you being patient, compassionate and kind? Are you focused on being present and are you determined to do what you set out to do? Are you "leading well"? Are you leading in service of others, rather than simply to bolster your own ego? If you find yourself leading from ego, stop for a moment to check what has triggered your insecurities. Every single person has insecurities; each one of us has a shadow side. The point is not to pretend they don't exist, but rather to welcome them and use this awareness to help to expand your wholeness, your humanity and to recognise that your imperfections are a gift to staying grounded and being humble.

Remember that you will not be able to manifest your dream and vision alone. You will need others to support you, to challenge you, to champion your vision and to help keep you on track. To inspire them to do this, show them what your dream looks like and invite them to dream with you. You will need to speak in a way that allows them to overcome their feelings of limitation and bias. They must be able to see what you see and be willing to go there with you. You should inspire them to follow you and make your dream theirs too. This is how leadership starts. You should also get to know the personal dreams and visions of those you are leading and do everything you can to encourage them to follow their own dreams too.

Leadership is hard work – it's constant work; it can also be sweaty and challenging. It's about rolling up your sleeves and jumping in, and doing the hard work. It's in your tears of frustration when you want to give up and your tears of gratitude when you see victory on the horizon. You will laugh and cry. You will throw in the towel and be encouraged to stand up again and get back into the ring. This is part of what leading well entails. You will learn resilience and you will persevere.

Leading well is very accessible; the principles are simple, as the elders I spoke to showed. The challenge is to truly understand them and to apply them. The greatest difficulty for many of us is to get off our high horses and surrender to the humility the learning process demands. Sticking to your principles and practising them every day also requires commitment and concentration.

There should be no difference between who we are and who we feel we are. Leadership is all about being the expression of what is in our true nature; it is how our values, our attitudes and our norms show up in the world as our behaviour. So to be able to lead well, we need to know who we are, what our values are, what we stand for and to have the courage and endurance to work towards fulfilling our dreams – our life's purpose in service of others.

All of us who believe in equality, fairness and humanity, aspire to social justice and to a world in which all people will be able to enjoy the same quality of peace, health and life opportunities as do the most fortunate in the world so they would not need to leave their homes to find it. We can work towards such a system one person at a time, one community at a time, one organisation at a time.

It is clear that we can't change the world over-night; we can't stop all conflict; we can't single-handedly take our communities out of poverty; or create new opportunities in our nations. One thing we can do is to share ideas and reflect on how we can co-create a future that we hope to have in twenty, fifty or a hundred years from now. We can plant the seeds of a better life for our children, our grandchildren and our great-grandchildren. Imagine if we each commit to working on this. What stands in our way? What will it take us to collectively transform it into sustainable development? To co-create the future with the intention of improving the lives of future generations, we should work to continue the efforts our ancestors started.

Throughout my youth I wondered why some people have to leave their countries and settle in a land that might not welcome them. Why do we have to find opportunities elsewhere and why are we unable to create those same opportunities at home? How long will I have to answer to those asking me where I am from? What will it take to allow people not to be forced to migrate, but to allow them to make a life right where they are?

I refuse to stop entertaining the idea that in my own small way I can help to change people's mindsets to unlock the leader in them. We can each do this anywhere in the world. I know that it is possible and that in so doing we each hold the possibilities and potential to transform the world, one person at a time.

X

WHAT NOW?

'What now?' was the question I asked myself as a ten-year-old wrenched from my life in Ethiopia all those years ago. I now know that the answer is to start by allowing optimism to emerge. Always remember that our reality is directly related to our thoughts and values. A better tomorrow is possible. We should all keep bolstering our optimism, particularly in these times of uncertainty. Optimism is a necessary discipline. It's so easy to become disheartened when we see what is happening around us, but we must believe that things are going to get better and that we do have the power to improve things.

Whenever I become discouraged, I think of this quote: 'Even if I knew that tomorrow the world would go to pieces, I would still plant my apple tree.' To me it means we should persist as if our dreams and visions will be realised. This is hope. Even though we may not be alive to see its fruits, we can still initiate change. We must be optimistic enough to plant the seeds of our aspirations, to nurture them and watch them grow, even if we know we may not be here tomorrow.

The truth is that none of us knows what is around the corner, nothing is guaranteed.

We should always remain hopeful and positive; if we go around in a pessimistic funk, we will only be able to imagine a negative outcome. The minute you direct your thoughts away from heaviness, the quality of those thoughts will start changing for the better. Your perspectives will improve and you will begin to see opportunities where once you only saw challenges. When I notice my thoughts veering off the sunny path, I try to coax them back by thinking of three things I am grateful for.

Once we accept both the endlessness and impermanence of time we will be able to slow down our thoughts and actions, to allow us to take true and firm steps forward in our lives. This understanding opens us up to our wisdom and insights and will allow us to transform.

We have seen this happen, for instance when children and adolescents all over the world, led by, amongst others, Swedish climate activist Greta Thunberg and Vanessa Nakate from Uganda, began speaking out on climate change issues. We have witnessed the growth of the Me Too movement bringing global attention to the abuse of women. We have watched the strengthening of the Black Lives Matter campaign throughout the world. We see people becoming increasingly vocal against injustice and human rights violations wherever they encounter them. It may not always feel like it's enough to stem the tide of growing racism, sexism and fascism, but it's happening and slowly we can see how the voice of each person does indeed count.

We have been given a basket of lessons handed to us by leaders who have inspired us, the elders who have come before and who employed these principles to help transform their corners of the world. I include in these lessons the many handed down personally to each of us from our own grandparents and other elders. We can choose to follow their teachings as we try to do better in our own lives and in our own leadership. We can practise them and build them into our own style of leadership, knowing that our actions will add to millions more carried out for the good of others.

Most of the leaders I interviewed said they were inspired by their belief in equality and a shared humanity and that is what got them started on their journey to transform the world into a more humane one. They had set themselves a vision to bring about change and transformation to the best of their ability. They accepted their responsibility as individuals and as part of a collective to do whatever they could to change the future so that it would be better for those coming after them. For each of them, it was not about whether they would be around to see this improved world; they planted the seeds of change and nurtured them because they had hope – they believed there was a chance that it would work.

What I have learned is that where we see injustice and suffering we don't need to wait for good leaders to take us out of it. We can all be leaders; we can all help to bring about change and transformation. Covid-19 has shown us that we have the tools to exchange information, knowledge and strategies, used now much more than we did before. The pandemic has opened our eyes to new ways of doing things. With the help of technology we can more easily start collaborating, pooling our energies and ideas across towns, cities, across nations and throughout the world. If we have Wi-Fi there is little to stop us from reaching out further than our own traditional groups and organisations, to help us connect with like-minded people in our quests for lasting change.

Whatever it is that moves us to want to change and improve upon as we serve others, we can remember to follow the principles of the elders. They are Dignity, Patience, Choice, Presence and Persistence.

Always treat people with dignity. You cannot treat people as worthless and expect to lead well. I work with team leaders and executives all over the world. Some of them, I have discovered, seem to think that just because they are the head of a team or a manager of this or manager of that, that they have a licence to mistreat people. No, that does not make you a leader. Mistreating people, be they your staff, your service providers or anyone else, does not make you a leader. What makes you a leader is when you treat people with dignity because they are human beings. Every person you encounter is somebody's son, somebody's daughter; they too have a family; they too have friends who love them. They too are important; they too are capable. So remember that Dignity is number one.

Patience. All the leaders I spoke to were patient. They were patient with me; they were patient with others and they were patient with the pace of change. They listened carefully and intently when someone else spoke and they were slow to respond. Patience is a habit and it allows us to make space for silence. I am sure you can think of a few managers who say, 'I have an open door policy, absolutely, I'm there to listen.' Are they really there? The minute you start a meeting with some of them you can't even put a word on the table. You see their attention wander and you hear them offering their views before they have even listened to yours. You know how this makes you feel; so when you are in that position, listen, because when you listen you create the possibility to understand what's being said, and what is unsaid. It is this understanding that is going to help you know how to lead, know how to serve, and it will open up all kinds of possibilities. Unless you listen you cannot serve. It's that simple.

Part of treating people with dignity and having patience is to be fair. When you're in a leadership position people look to you to set the standard. People look up to you; so be fair, be objective. Don't do something because you favour somebody or you don't favour something. Be fair, because when you're fair, the people around you are fair; it's infectious. When the people around you are fair you create a fair system. When you create a fair system you have a fair culture and you can move forward together with ease. It's not about who you know; it's about what you do and how you make people feel. You get out what you put in. You can't not be fair. If somebody shows up late all the time, figure out why they are showing up late. Figure it out; don't just say, 'it's okay'. It's not okay; be fair, and treat everybody equally.

Just as you are slow to respond, also be slow to reprimand. Being a leader does not entitle you to punish people and to reprimand them as if it's food for your ego. Be careful because when you're in a leadership position, you can become blinded by power and you might start thinking you're some sort of God. It's not true. We're not God, so be slow to reprimand. Reprimanding someone should be a conversation to help them to correct their behaviour so they can get back on track. You can't do that by humiliating them. Be slow to reprimand.

Be Present. Focus on what you are doing, don't be sidetracked into something else. Be mindful about what is happening around you, what is being said and how you respond. Live with awareness and treat those around you like they matter; really matter. When they have something to say let them say it. Drop your multitasking and listen to them carefully.

Remember that you have choice; choice is your super-power. You can make that decision to act with dignity and to treat others with dignity; you choose to listen with intent; you can choose how to respond or how not to respond. These choices give you control. They allow you to respond intentionally instead of resorting to a default knee-jerk response.

Build your own resilience, be persistent, keep going despite the potholes and bumps along the way, especially the human shaped ones. You have chosen your purpose and your vision; stay the course until you have achieved what your heart desires.

The last thing to remember is to take time for reflection; build it into your daily programme. If you don't, you are going to lose track of what's important and what's not important. Every day my grandmother woke up around four thirty a.m. and she just sat, for meditation and for prayer for at least two hours. This is what gave her the distance for the day. This is where you will get your guidance. And maybe you do it by taking a walk every morning or afternoon. However you choose to do it, please take time to reflect. When you are clear about your purpose and clear about how you treat people, the axis goes to the highest level of leadership. This is how you lead well. And you know why it's easy to lead well? Because you end up leading with your heart.

ACKNOWLEDGEMENTS

'If you want to go fast, go alone; if you want to go far, go together.' This African proverb best captures how thankful I am for all my family wide and far, all my dear friends around the world, and my huge community of amazing women, my girlfriends. Throughout my life, every step forward I have made, despite my doubts, fears, uncertainty and hardships, was only possible because, no matter where I was, we remained together in spirit. It gave me immense courage; allowed me to get up again every time I fell; to keep believing and to never feel lonely. I owe you everything. Knowing you are there, feeling your love and encouragement made it okay for me to keep walking even when I could not see the path ahead. I feel immense gratitude to God for having blessed me with so many friends, men and women of all ages, all ethnicities, all faiths and from all sorts of life journeys. This is the kind of wealth one can't put in the bank, but it makes all the difference in life.

No child is born with an owner's manual. There is no such thing as perfect parenting. Many of us might not fully grasp the sacrifices that our parents have made for us. But there comes a time – a moment of reverence – when one realises it. I have dedicated this book to my parents, my mother Selamawit Makonnen and my father Assegid Tessema. Life has certainly not been easy for you; you have faced so many trials and tribulations. Despite them you have remained kind, loving and always committed to us. I am so grateful to have you in my life and blessed that you are my parents. I have learned from your hard work, discipline, perseverance and determination.

My Aunt Elisabeth Makonnen, aka Koky, has supported me and called me almost every day as she always does and also through the process of writing this book. Kokiyé, you are my guardian angel and my mentor. Thank you for all that you have done for me. Like Koky, my Aunt Elene Makonnen has been with me every step of the way, helping me brainstorm ideas, discussing issues and keeping me encouraged.

None of this would have happened without the support of my daughters, Rosi-Selam and Leoni-Almaz. You are so much more than my daughters, you have become my girlfriends and sisters. Thank you so much for all that you have done for me, and for your constant support and encouragement. I miss you every day but I am grateful and so happy that you are following your dreams and studying what you love. Whatever makes you happy makes me happy.

Matthias Reusing, my life partner, my soulmate, my husband, thank you for all that you are; thank you for making us discover the world through your geographer and environmentalist lens. I learn so much with you, every day. Thank you for all your support and thank you for letting me do what I do. We are in this journey together. All the research in this book would have never happened without your loving support.

To all the leaders, who welcomed me, who gave me their precious time and who believed in my work, I am beyond honoured. I am grateful for all that you have shared with me and taught me. I will do my very best to share what you have given me with as many people as I possibly can.

I would like to mention Adriana Marais, Alice Mockel, Alix Drummond, Annie Nut, Badjeba Tekle-Tsadik, Béatrice Arnaud, Bénédicte Ausset, Bernadette Verhaeghe, Carola Fuentes, Claire-Noelle Jamoulle, Darija Lali, Deborah Boyar, Faye Yu, Fofi Assegid, Fouad Ismaël, Hope Chigudu, Jessica Horn, Joanne Gozawa, Joséphine Ouedraogo, Judy Lendzian, Kelo Kubu, Kidist Wossene, Larry Biel, Laura Johnson, Lily Assegid, Liu Feifei, Lole Tasco, Losane Dehne Retta, Martine Shahbazian, Michael and Maureen McMurphy, Morag Carolan, Ndye Njie, Nestanet Mesfin, Noela Assegid, Ono Batkhuu, Patty de León Toledo, Paula Fray, Philippe and Zakia Legrand, Priscilla Achapka, Priscilla Banda, Rahel Terrefe, Rama Rothe, Rania Duri, Rita Mazzocchi, Saima Butt, Sally

Yeh, Stephanie McGuire, Sylvia Sage, Teguest Yilma, Teresa Woodland, Tim Kemp, Tine Veldkamp, Violet Drummond, and all the Sisters at Daughters of Charity Ethiopia. Even though you had no idea I was working on this book and pulling long nights in writing, your calls and all the conversations we shared gave me light, energy and encouraged me all along the way. Thank you for so much more than words can describe.

Sahm Venter, my editor – are there enough words to describe our relationship and what you are in my life? You are a soulmate, a sister, a bestie, and on top of that, a master at your trade. You are a needle in a haystack. Heaven must have been smiling on me the day we met. I cannot imagine my life without our sisterhood, let alone working without you. May the Heavens whisper to you how much you mean to me, because it would take me days to find the words.

To my grandmother, Lady Almaz Haile-Mariam, "aka Almazesha", even though you are no longer with us here on earth, you are with us in spirit all the time. I see you in the sunrise, you talk to me in my dreams, I see your smile in the morning dew, and in times of darkness, my thoughts of you are whispers guiding me. You remain my soul's lighthouse.

Last but not least, I thank The Lord for making this book possible, for inspiring me and for allowing me to feel His presence in my life every single day.

ABOUT THE AUTHOR

Yene Assegid was born in Ethiopia and raised in Europe. She completed her tertiary education in the United States where she earned a Bachelor of Business Administration, an MBA and a PhD in Humanities.

A Master Certified Coach, she works as a Transformational Leadership Coach supporting leaders, managers, and teams in the corporate world, in international development institutions and civil society organisations around the world. In 2020, she established the Everyones World Leadership Foundation (ELF) Program, an online leadership development and coaching initiative for young women.

She lives in Lusaka, Zambia with her husband Matthias Reusing. Their daughters Rosi and Leoni are studying abroad.

Leading with Heart
Yene Assegid

Other titles by Yene Assegid
Butterflies over Africa: Perspectives on Changing and Transforming the Continent
(Integral Publishers, 2009)
Forget not the Sparrows: Unfinished Conversations with My Grandmother
(Shola Stories, 2011)
Shine: Re-Scripting your Life in Partnership with the Universe (2017)

First published by the author in 2021

The author is grateful for literary permissions to reproduce items subject to copyright. Every effort has been made to trace the copyright holders and the author apologises for any unintentional omission. The author would be pleased to hear from anyone not acknowledged here and undertakes to make all reasonable efforts to include the appropriate acknowledgement in any subsequent editions: p. 7: author unknown; p. 58: Nelson Mandela, from a letter to K. D. Matanzima dated 14 October 1968, *The Prison Letters of Nelson Mandela*, Ed. Sahm Venter (New York, USA: Liveright Publishing Corporation, a division of W. W. Norton & Company, 2018), copyright © 2018 by the Estate of Nelson Rolihlahla Mandela and the Nelson Mandela Foundation; p. 72: author unknown (but widely attributed to Friedrich Nietzsche); p. 93: Martin Luther, date unknown.

ISBN: 978-0-9885792-7-9

Cover design by Cameron Gibb
Editing by Sahm Venter
Proofreading by David Carles
Author portrait by Qian Ma, Imagine Photography Studio
Design and typesetting by Blackwell & Ruth